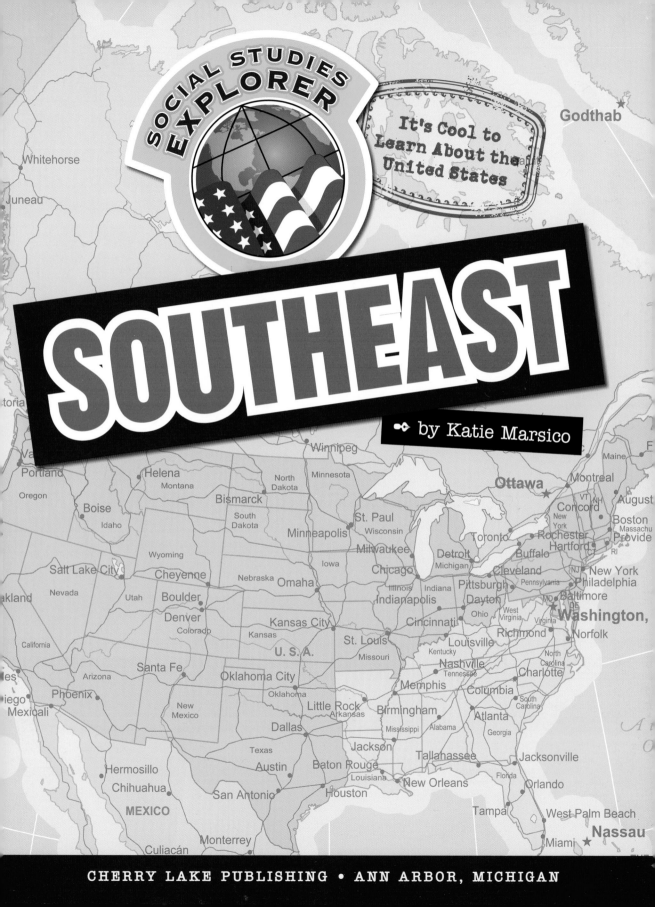

SOCIAL STUDIES EXPLORER

It's Cool to Learn About the United States

SOUTHEAST

❧ by Katie Marsico

CHERRY LAKE PUBLISHING • ANN ARBOR, MICHIGAN

Published in the United States of America
by Cherry Lake Publishing
Ann Arbor, Michigan
www.cherrylakepublishing.com

Content Adviser: James Wolfinger, PhD, Associate Professor,
History and Teacher Education, DePaul University, Chicago, Illinois

Book design: The Design Lab

Photo credits: Cover and page 3, ©iStockphoto.com/gchutka, ©iStockphoto.
com/killahfunkadelic, ©iStockphoto.com/gelyngfjell, and ©Yuri Tuchkov/
Shutterstock, Inc.; page 4, ©Tom Denham/Dreamstime.com; page 5, ©Matt
Antonino/Dreamstime.com; page 6, ©Michael Pettigrew/Dreamstime.
com; page 8, ©Rob Byron/Shutterstock, Inc.; page 9, ©Stevebrigman/
Dreamstime.com; page 10, ©Ron Chapple Studios/Dreamstime.com; page
11, ©Lunamarina/Dreamstime.com; page 12, ©Jeff Kinsey/Dreamstime.
com; page 13, ©Chrisseman/Dreamstime.com; page 14, ©Designpicssub/
Dreamstime.com; page 15, ©Greg Amptman/Dreamstime.com; pages
16, 17, 18, and 23, ©North Wind Picture Archives/Alamy; page 21,
©thatsmymop/Shutterstock, Inc.; page 22, ©C. Kurt Holter/Shutterstock,
Inc.; page 24, ©Martin Thomas Photography/Alamy; page 26, ©Lbarn/
Dreamstime.com; page 27, ©Joseph Sohm-Visions of America/Media
Bakery; page 28, ©Fotoluminate/Dreamstime.com; page 29, ©Olivier Le
Queinec/Dreamstime.com; page 30, ©Joe Gough/Shutterstock, Inc.; page 32,
©Steve Heap/Shutterstock, Inc.; page 33, ©Steve Kingsman/Dreamstime.
com; page 34, ©Philip Lange/Shutterstock, Inc.; page 35, ©Kenneth D
Durden/Dreamstime.com; page 36, ©Juan Moyano/Dreamstime.com; page
37, ©Reika/Shutterstock, Inc.; page 38, ©3445128471/Shutterstock, Inc.;
40, ©Mark Stout Photography/Shutterstock, Inc.; page 41, ©Cafebeanz
Company/Dreamstime.com; page 42, ©Jose Gil/Dreamstime.com; page
43©Mike Flippo/Shutterstock, Inc.

Library of Congress Cataloging-in-Publication Data
Marsico, Katie, 1980–
    It's cool to learn about the United States: Southeast/by Katie Marsico.
        p. cm.—(Social studies explorer)
    Includes bibliographical references and index.
    ISBN-13: 978-1-61080-181-2 (lib. bdg.)
    ISBN-13: 978-1-61080-303-8 (pbk.)
    1. Southern States—Juvenile literature. I. Title. II. Title: Southeast. III.
Series.
    F209.3.M37 2011
    975—dc22   2011006971

Cherry Lake Publishing would like to acknowledge the work
of The Partnership for 21st Century Skills. Please visit
www.21stcenturyskills.org for more information.

Printed in the United States of America
Corporate Graphics Inc.
July 2011
CLFA09

SOUTHEAST

TABLE OF CONTENTS

USA FIRST-CLASS FOREVER

CHAPTER ONE

WELCOME TO THE SOUTHEAST

➥ There are many beaches along Florida's coast.

Would you like to hike through Arkansas's Ozark Mountains? Maybe you would prefer to hunt for sea-shells along a Florida beach. Perhaps U.S. history is your thing, and you would rather visit a famous battle site in

Virginia. Just be sure you have enough time left over to enjoy a little country music in Tennessee and a steaming bowl of **gumbo** in Louisiana!

The Southeast is made up of 12 states: Alabama, Arkansas, Florida, Georgia, Kentucky, Louisiana, Mississippi, North Carolina, South Carolina, Tennessee, Virginia, and West Virginia. In 2009, about 78,320,977 people lived in this region.

➻ Nashville, Tennessee, is known as the home of the country music industry.

➤ The Potomac River runs through West Virginia, Virginia, Maryland, and Washington, DC.

THE LAY OF THE LAND

The geography of the Southeast is as diverse as the people who live there. Kentucky is filled with short, steep hills and flat highlands called plateaus. The Mississippi River flows along its western border. The Appalachian Mountains tower over eastern Kentucky, as well as West Virginia and Virginia. Thick forests and deep caves fill the landscape in this portion of the Southeast. In Virginia, the James, Potomac, Rappahannock, and York Rivers flow into Chesapeake Bay, which empties into the Atlantic Ocean.

ACTIVITY

STATE CAPITALS

Make a copy of this map of the United States. The southeastern states are yellow. Each star represents the location of a state capital. Look at the list to the right of the map and write the names of the capitals next to the stars in the correct states.

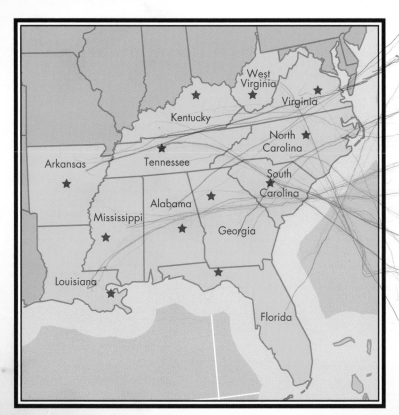

Montgomery
Little Rock
Tallahassee
Atlanta
Frankfort
Baton Rouge
Jackson
Raleigh
Columbia
Nashville
Richmond
Charleston

Answers: Alabama, Montgomery; Arkansas, Little Rock; Florida, Tallahassee; Georgia, Atlanta; Kentucky, Frankfort; Louisiana, Baton Rouge; Mississippi, Jackson; North Carolina, Raleigh; South Carolina, Columbia; Tennessee, Nashville; Virginia, Richmond; West Virginia, Charleston

Farther south, low-lying coastal plains stretch across eastern North Carolina and South Carolina. An area known as the Piedmont makes up the middle sections of these states. It is shaped by several plateaus and foothills. The Appalachian Mountains spread across the western portion of the Carolinas. They rise over much of eastern Tennessee, too. Forests cover many of that state's mountain ridges and sloping hillsides.

The Mississippi River forms Tennessee's western border, helping to create **fertile** soil that is good for farming. This river flows across other parts of the Southeast as

➥ The Appalachians form one of the longest mountain ranges in the country.

⊷ The Ozarks contain many beautiful waterfalls.

well, including eastern Arkansas. The Ozark and Ouachita Mountains cut through the northwestern and west central portions of that state. Like Tennessee, Arkansas is filled with thick woods and fertile plains and valleys. It is also famous for its many caves, **gorges**, and **springs**.

Louisiana, directly south of Arkansas, has several well-known geographic features. One of these is the Mississippi River delta. A delta is a low triangular area that is made from soil and rock that builds up when a river divides or empties into a larger body of water. The Mississippi River delta sits where the Mississippi River

☜ The wetlands of the Southeast are home to many plant and animal species.

flows into the Gulf of Mexico. It contains Louisiana's richest farmlands. Marshes, swamps, and **bayous** also make up the state's landscape.

Mississippi lies just to the east of Louisiana, Arkansas, and the Mississippi River. In addition to its fertile plains, Mississippi is filled with steep banks called bluffs, sandy hills, forests, and prairies. It is bordered by the Gulf of Mexico to the south. Alabama and Georgia are also located along the gulf. The southern portions of these states are mainly made up of coastal plains that feature everything from swamps to pine forests. The Piedmont stretches across the middle of Alabama and Georgia. The hills, plateaus, and valleys of the Appalachian Mountains cover the states' northern sections.

Most of Florida is surrounded by the Gulf of Mexico, a narrow channel of water known as the Florida Straits, and the Atlantic Ocean. Low hills, lakes, and forests are common to the northwest. Coastal plains spread over eastern and southern Florida. They are the site of several marshes and swamps, including the Everglades.

A large chain of islands called the Florida Keys curve away from the bottom tip of mainland Florida. The Keys loop in a southwestern direction and are located in the Florida Straits. They include a total of 1,700 islands.

WEATHER WATCH

The Southeast experiences a variety of climates. People who live in northern parts of the Southeast tend to experience cold winters and warm summers that can sometimes become quite hot. The weather changes slightly as you head farther south. Much of the Southeast's climate is described as subtropical. This means that summers are usually hot and **humid**, and winters are generally cool and mild. Southern Florida has a tropical climate, so the weather is typically warm and wet all year long.

➡ Thunderstorms are common in the Southeast.

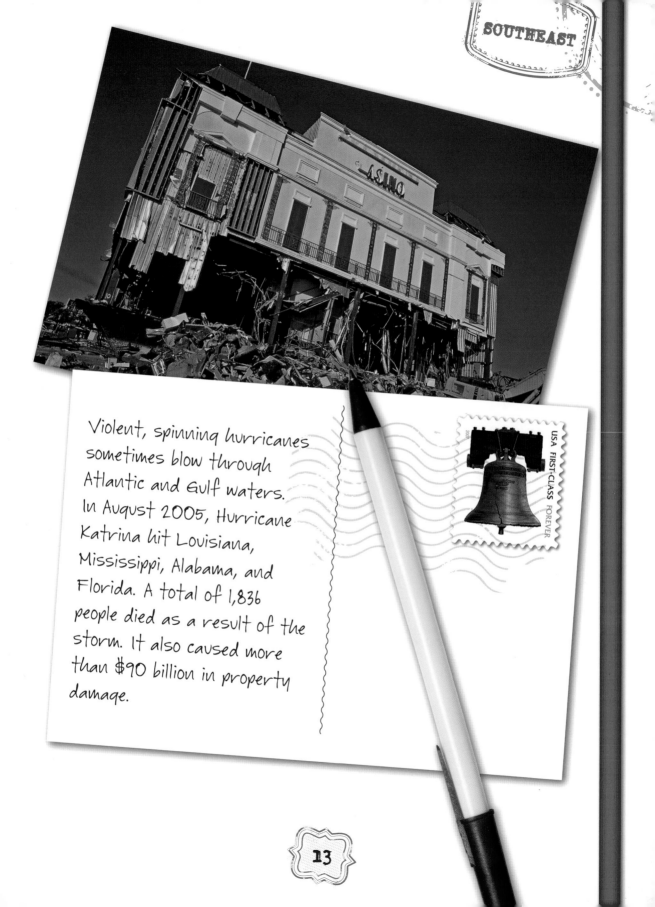

Violent, spinning hurricanes sometimes blow through Atlantic and Gulf waters. In August 2005, Hurricane Katrina hit Louisiana, Mississippi, Alabama, and Florida. A total of 1,836 people died as a result of the storm. It also caused more than $90 billion in property damage.

USA FIRST-CLASS FOREVER

PLANTS AND WILDLIFE

Countless species of plants and animals make the Southeast their home. Gray wolves, red foxes, black bears, and panthers live there. Bobcats, alligators, and bald eagles can also be found in the Southeast. Plants in this region include everything from pines and palm trees to buttercups and water lilies.

➥ Wolves are common in some parts of the southeast.

→ Scientists are studying the lifespan of sea turtles. Some species live for an average of 80 years.

Unfortunately, some southeastern species are endangered. Overhunting and destruction to the environment have put them at serious risk. West Indian manatees and various kinds of sea turtles and whales that swim off southeastern shores are endangered. So are gray bats, wood storks, and several varieties of white-tailed deer. Hundreds of trees and flowers, including many types of willows, myrtles, cedars, and orchids, are also endangered.

CHAPTER TWO

A RICH HISTORY

➮ The Seminole settled in Florida long ago. Some members of this group still live there.

The history of the Southeast region dates back about 12,000 years. This is the earliest that historians believe Native Americans began living in the area. Several native peoples resided in the Southeast, including Cherokee, Choctaw, Creek, and Seminole. They fished in coastal waters and hunted in the region's thick forests.

They also learned to grow crops such as beans and maize (corn) on the rolling plains.

Life changed for many Native Americans when European **colonists** began to arrive in the Southeast in the early 1600s. In 1607, Great Britain established its first permanent settlement at Jamestown, Virginia. Between that time and 1732, England settled 12 other colonies in what is now the United States. Georgia, North Carolina, and South Carolina were among those original colonies. Throughout the 18th and early 19th centuries, the British,

➥ British colonists arrived in Jamestown, Virginia, in 1607.

Spanish, and French claimed control over much of present-day Alabama, Arkansas, and Florida. They also claimed Kentucky, Louisiana, Mississippi, Tennessee, and West Virginia.

European colonists gradually pushed Native Americans off their land. Between the 17th and 18th centuries, most southeastern tribes were forced west of the Mississippi River. The colonists were eager to use former Native American territories for farming, hunting, mining, and the development of towns and cities.

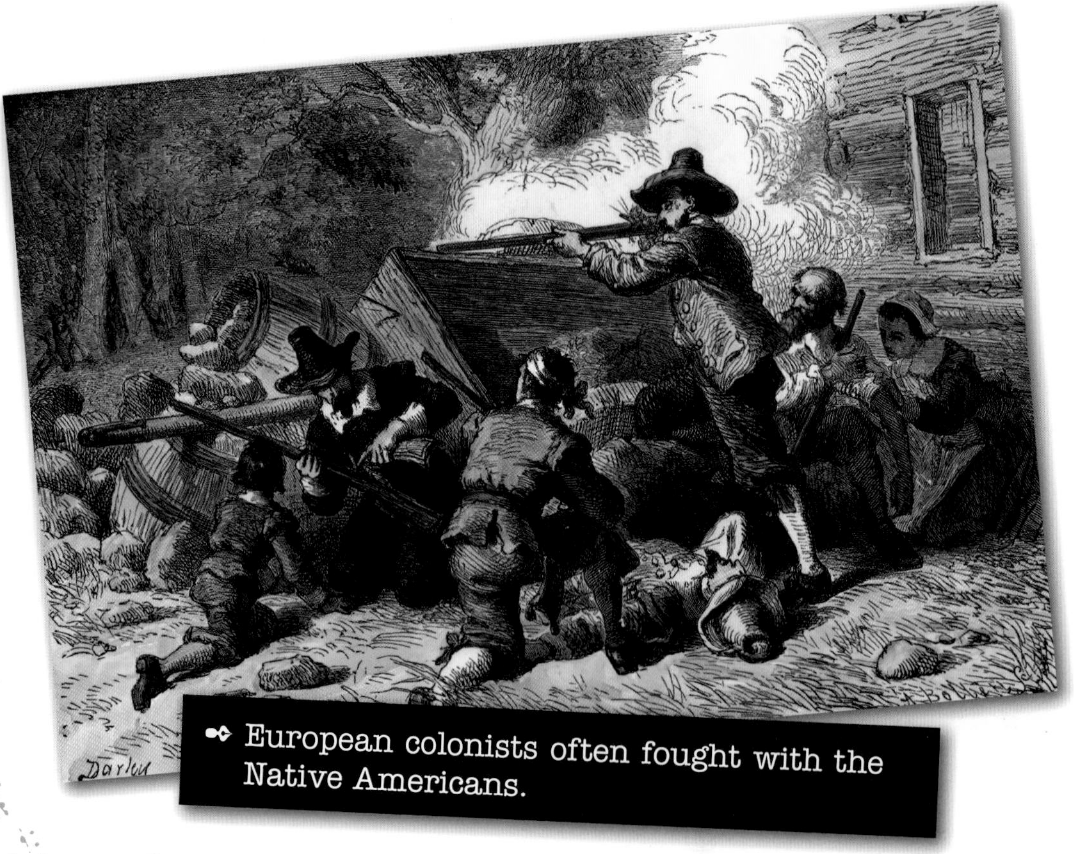

European colonists often fought with the Native Americans.

In 1838 and 1839, the U.S. government forced 15,000 Cherokee Indians living in Georgia to move west of the Mississippi River. Starvation and sickness caused the deaths of about 5,000 men, women, and children who traveled westward. Their journey is known as the Trail of Tears.

AN INDEPENDENT NATION

By 1775, many British subjects who had settled in America wanted to break free from the control of England. They battled for and won their independence by defeating Great Britain in the American Revolutionary War (1775–1783).

After the war ended, the 13 original colonies became states in the **union** called the United States of America. U.S. officials began purchasing lands from Spain and France. Between the late 1790s and early 1820s, the United States gained control of territories that were eventually carved into five states. The land became the states of Louisiana, Mississippi, Alabama, Arkansas, and Florida. In 1863, West Virginia was the last southeastern state to join the Union.

States in the Southeast officially achieved statehood on the following dates:

STATE	DATE OF STATEHOOD	STATE NUMBER
Georgia	January 2, 1788	4th
South Carolina	May 23, 1788	8th
Virginia	June 25, 1788	10th
North Carolina	November 21, 1789	12th
Kentucky	June 1, 1792	15th
Tennessee	June 1, 1796	16th
Louisiana	April 30, 1812	18th
Mississippi	December 10, 1817	20th
Alabama	December 14, 1819	22nd
Arkansas	June 15, 1836	25th
Florida	March 3, 1845	27th
West Virginia	June 20, 1863	35th

→ Abraham Lincoln was the president of the United States during the Civil War.

AN ENDANGERED UNION

By the time West Virginia entered the Union, many southeastern states had already broken away from it. In 1860 and 1861, 11 states—South Carolina, Mississippi, Florida, Alabama, Georgia, Louisiana, Texas, Virginia, Arkansas, North Carolina, and Tennessee—**seceded** from the Union. They withdrew because they feared President Abraham Lincoln and other U.S. leaders would end slavery.

Since early colonial times, a large number of white southerners had relied upon African slaves to work on large farms called plantations. Most people who lived in northern states believed that slavery denied the freedoms and rights that all Americans deserved. This issue divided the country and led to the outbreak of the American Civil War (1861–1865).

States that seceded joined together to form a separate government called the Confederate States of America, or the Confederacy. Those that remained loyal to the United States fought for the Union. Kentucky never seceded, but many of its residents continued to support slavery.

⟶ Many Civil War battlegrounds are now national historic sites.

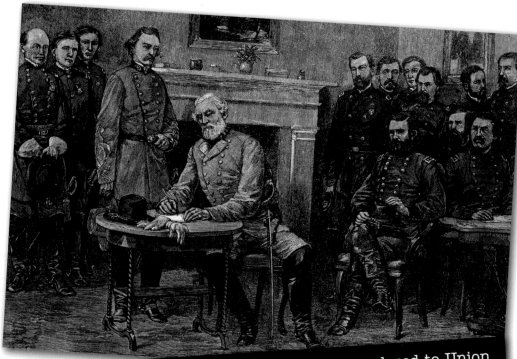

•❖ Confederate general Robert E. Lee surrendered to Union general Ulysses S. Grant at Appomattox, Virginia.

Meanwhile, West Virginia was created when some of the people who lived in Virginia opposed that state's decision to withdraw from the Union.

In April 1865, Confederate forces surrendered in Appomattox, Virginia. Over the next 5 years, states that had supported the Confederacy reentered the Union. The U.S. government also created laws that ended slavery and granted African Americans new rights as citizens. Yet it would be almost a century before many African Americans actually received equal treatment.

⊶ The Civil Rights Museum in Memphis, Tennessee, features an exhibit on the Montgomery Bus Boycott.

People who were involved in the civil rights movement during the 1950s and 1960s participated in marches and protests to fight for racial equality. Several famous events connected to this movement took place in the Southeast. For example, African Americans in Montgomery, Alabama, made history in 1955 and 1956. They **boycotted** city buses that forced blacks and whites to sit in separate areas.

FAMOUS SOUTHERNERS

Can you match the names of the following southerners to what made them famous?

NAME	ACCOMPLISHMENT AND HOME STATE
1. Pocahontas	a. Third U.S. president and longtime resident of Virginia
2. Robert E. Lee	b. Civil rights activist who helped begin the Montgomery Bus Boycott
3. Rosa Parks	c. Native American princess who aided Jamestown colonists
4. Sequoya	d. Leader of the Confederate forces during the Civil War
5. Thomas Jefferson	e. Southeastern Cherokee Indian who developed a written language for his tribe

Answers: 1-c; 2-d; 3-b; 4-e; 5-a

CHAPTER THREE

GOVERNMENT AND ECONOMY

➤ South Carolina's capitol is the city of Columbia.

Most of the state governments that exist throughout the Southeast are similar to those found in other parts of the country. Like the U.S. government, state governments are broken into three main branches: legislative, executive, and judicial.

GOVERNMENT AT WORK

The legislative branch in each state usually features two houses, a senate and a house of representatives. In Virginia and West Virginia, the House of Representatives is called the House of Delegates. Voters in each state elect the representatives, whose job is to make or change state laws.

The executive branch is headed by a governor, who is in charge of making sure that state laws are carried out. The governor typically works alongside other members of the executive branch, including a lieutenant governor,

◆◆ Virginia's House of Delegates met in the Old Hall of the House of Delegates from 1788 to 1904.

an attorney general, and a secretary of state. Groups of executive managers, or commissioners, oversee state issues ranging from education to transportation.

The judicial branch of most state governments is controlled by a supreme court. Judges who serve on this court make rulings, or official decisions, that are meant to settle questions or issues related to state laws.

Each state is divided into smaller units of government districts called counties. Many of these counties are often

➥ Florida's state supreme court meets in this building.

made up of cities, towns, and villages. Local governments throughout the Southeast are mostly organized the same way as they are in other parts of the country.

Louisiana is not broken into counties. Instead, residents live in 64 districts called parishes. There is no difference between parishes and counties. But the word parish dates back to the Spanish and French colonists who once resided in Louisiana. Many of the settlers who came from Spain and France were Roman Catholics. Members of this religion belong to church communities known as parishes. When U.S. officials organized the lands that made up Louisiana, the districts they created fell along the same borders as local Roman Catholic parishes.

A VIBRANT ECONOMY

Workers in the Southeast supply the rest of the nation and foreign countries with a wide variety of goods and services. Agriculture plays a major role in southeastern business. About 46 percent of the rice harvested in the United States comes from Arkansas. Georgia farmers are the nation's leading growers of peanuts and pecans. Both states are the country's top producers of young chickens called broilers. Many southeastern farmers also raise cotton, tobacco, soybeans, and sugarcane. They also raise oranges, peaches, and beef and dairy cattle.

➥ Farming is a major part of the economy of the Southeast.

MISSISSIPPI EXPORTS

Use the following information to create a bar graph. Your graph will show how different types of Mississippi farm products contributed to the total value of agricultural exports in 2009. Which bar do you predict will be the longest? Which do you think will be the shortest?

- Mississippi farmers **exported** more than $4 million in farm products.
- The sale of broilers made up about 49 percent of this number.
- Profits from soybean farming represented slightly more than 16 percent.
- Roughly 8 percent of the value was connected to corn sales.

The state of West Virginia is second in coal production in the United States. Only Wyoming produces more coal each year.

Other types of industries also drive the region's economy. Virginia and West Virginia are famous for their coal mines, a vital source of energy. Other southeastern states such as Alabama and Tennessee are well-known for manufacturing automobiles. North Carolina is home to the world's largest scientific research center, Research Triangle Park. Dozens of high-tech companies are located in or near the park.

Tourism is also an important industry in the Southeast. Men and women who work in theme parks such as Disney World are examples of southerners who have service jobs. Service workers provide services instead of producing specific goods. Restaurant, hotel, and shop employees are other examples of service workers.

➙ Disney World in Orlando, Florida, is a popular tourist attraction.

CHAPTER FOUR

A MIX OF PEOPLE AND CULTURES

↝ The city of Miami, Florida, has a diverse population of more than 400,000 people.

There are many things you might find interesting about the southeastern United States. As you read on, however, you may discover that the people who call this region home are the main reason it is so appealing.

A RAINBOW OF CULTURES

African Americans have contributed a lot to southerners' cultural identities. In some southeastern states, African Americans make up about 36 percent of the population. Many African Americans who reside in the Southeast today have ancestors who worked there as slaves hundreds of years ago. During the 18th and 19th centuries, these men and women often sang religious songs called spirituals. Spirituals remain popular throughout the Southeast today.

◦◦ New Orleans has a rich musical tradition.

Many people who live in the Southeast can trace their roots to Spanish-speaking countries. In some southeastern states such as Florida, Latinos and Hispanics make up about 16 percent of the population. One well-known neighborhood in Miami is called Little Havana because of the large number of residents who originally came from Havana, Cuba.

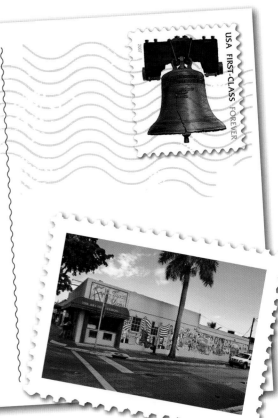

MUSIC AND FOOD

African Americans also played an important role in introducing blues and jazz to the region during the early 1900s. Yet these are not the only types of music that reflect the culture of the Southeast. Countless **bluegrass** and country hits have come out of southeastern states such as Kentucky, Tennessee, Virginia, and West Virginia. Bristol, Tennessee, is frequently called the Birthplace of Country Music because country songs were first commercially recorded there.

The traditional foods also say a lot about southeastern culture. Many of the Cajun and Creole dishes that are commonly served in Louisiana are influenced by French cooking styles. This is partly due to the large number of French colonists who once settled in the area. Gumbo and jambalaya are popular Cajun and Creole foods. Jambalaya is a spicy rice dish that usually contains sausage or shellfish and tomatoes, peppers, onions, and celery.

•◇ You can find many southeastern recipes for jambalaya.

Southerners are also famous for their barbecued meats and fried chicken. Fresh seafood is frequently served in coastal areas. For a tasty dessert, you will probably enjoy sampling pecan pie and bread pudding in several southeastern states. If you head to Florida, where farmers grow a variety of fresh citrus fruits, think about ordering a slice of mouthwatering key lime pie!

Fried chicken is a popular dish in many southeastern states.

Do you want to get a "taste" of Louisiana? Try this recipe for a pot of easy-to-make gumbo! Be sure to have an adult help you with the chopping and cooking.

Chicken Gumbo

INGREDIENTS

2 cups chopped okra
1 small onion, chopped
1/4 green pepper, chopped
1/2 stick butter
5 cups chicken broth
2 cups crushed tomatoes

1 bay leaf
1/4 teaspoon salt
1/4 teaspoon pepper
1/2 cup rice
1 cup diced cooked chicken
1 tablespoon parsley

→ Crackers go well with a bowl of hot chicken gumbo!

INSTRUCTIONS

1. Placed the chopped okra, onion, and green pepper in a bowl.

2. Melt the butter in a large pot on your stove top.

3. Add the chopped okra, onion, and green pepper to the pot. Allow to simmer for about 10 minutes or until the vegetables are tender.

4. Add the chicken broth, tomatoes, bay leaf, salt, and pepper to the pot. Continue to simmer.

5. Stir in the rice and cover the pot. Simmer for an additional 20 minutes.

6. Add the chicken and parsley to the pot. Cook until your gumbo is thoroughly heated (probably an extra 5 to 10 minutes). Remove the bay leaf before serving. You should have about 7 cups of this southeastern stew to share with family and friends!

FESTIVAL TIME

Mardi Gras in New Orleans, Louisiana, is perhaps the most famous celebration in the Southeast. The term *Mardi Gras* is French for "Fat Tuesday." Fat Tuesday usually falls in February or March, just before the beginning of Lent. This is a holy season in which Roman Catholics avoid eating certain foods or give up their favorite activities or comforts to focus on becoming more spiritually pure. On Fat Tuesday people have a final opportunity to enjoy themselves before Lent starts. In New Orleans,

➥ Colorful floats are a common sight at Mardi Gras parades.

residents and visitors participate in a citywide festival. It features parades, dancing, parties, contests, and colorful masks and costumes.

Other celebrations that occur throughout the Southeast include everything from reenactments of Civil War battles to annual car shows. Some events are related to yearly sports games. College football's Orange Bowl takes place every January at Sun Life Stadium in Miami Gardens, Florida. Watching or attending this college football competition is an important tradition for many people across the nation.

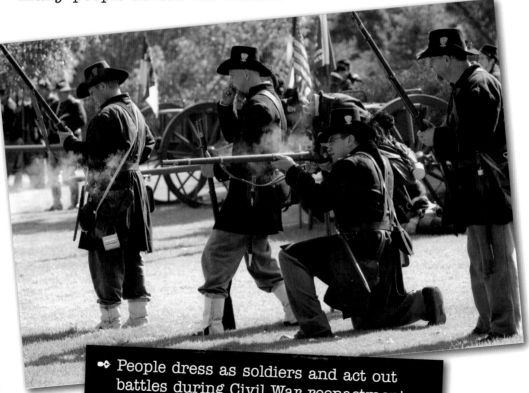

➥ People dress as soldiers and act out battles during Civil War reenactments.

◦→ Pecan pie is a traditional southeastern dessert.

Whether you are cheering in a Florida stadium or moving your feet to a bluegrass tune in Kentucky, you are sure to have fun celebrating life in the Southeast. You can look for sea turtles, explore the site of the earliest American colony, or dig into a slice of pecan pie. No matter where you turn, a new opportunity to learn about the southeastern United States is certain to add excitement to your journey!

FAST FACTS

Population (2009): 78,320,977

Total area of region: 555,177 square miles (1,437,902 square kilometers)

Highest point: 6,684 feet (2,037 meters) Mount Mitchell near Burnsville, North Carolina

Lowest point: 8 feet (2.4 m) below sea level in New Orleans, Louisiana

Highest recorded temperature: 120°F (49°C) on August 10, 1936, in Ozark, Arkansas

Lowest recorded temperature: -37°F (-38°C) in Shelbyville, Kentucky on January 19, 1994, and in Lewisburg, West Virginia, on December 30, 1917

Largest cities (2009): Jacksonville, Florida (813, 518); Charlotte, North Carolina (709, 441); Memphis, Tennessee (676,640); Nashville, Tennessee (605,473); Louisville, Kentucky (566,503)

Professional Sports Teams:

Major League Baseball: Atlanta Braves, Florida Marlins, and Tampa Bay Rays

National Basketball Association: Atlanta Hawks, Charlotte Bobcats, Memphis Grizzlies, Miami Heat, New Orleans Hornets, and Orlando Magic

National Football League: Atlanta Falcons, Carolina Panthers, Jacksonville Jaguars, Miami Dolphins, New Orleans Saints, Tampa Bay Buccaneers, and Tennessee Titans

National Hockey League: Carolina Hurricanes, Florida Panthers, Nashville Predators, and Tampa Bay Lightning

GLOSSARY

bayous (BYE-ooz) marshy wetlands

bluegrass (BLOO-gras) a type of fast country music that is often played on banjos and guitars

boycotted (BOI-kaht-ed) refused to pay for goods or services as a form of political protest

colonists (KA-luh-nists) people from another country who settle in a new land but who still keep ties to their home country

exported (EK-sport-ed) sold goods or services to another country

fertile (FUR-tuhl) capable of supporting rich plant growth

gorges (GORJ-iz) deep, narrow valleys with steep sides

gumbo (GUHM-bo) a thick okra stew

humid (HYOO-mid) containing warm, moist air

seceded (si-SEED-id) formally withdrew from a group or an organization

springs (SPRINGZ) natural flows of groundwater

union (YOON-yuhn) a political unit made up of formerly independent groups; when capitalized, Union refers to the United States of America

BOOKS

De Angelis, Gina. *Virginia*. New York: Children's Press, 2009.

Glaser, Jason. *Kentucky: The Bluegrass State*. New York: PowerKids Press, 2010.

Smith, Rich. *Georgia*. Edina, MN: ABDO Publishing Company, 2010.

WEB SITES

Harcourt School Publishers: Welcome to the Southeast
www.harcourtschool.com/ss1/adventure_activities/interactives/gr4_unit3.html
Visit this site for an interactive quiz on the southeastern United States.

Louisiana Kids Fun and Education Page
www.house.louisiana.gov/pubinfo/kids.htm
Scan this House of Representatives site for coloring pages, quizzes, maps, and games related to Louisiana.

North Carolina Secretary of State: Kids Page
www.secretary.state.nc.us/kidspg/
Explore this site for games, fun facts, and photos that will help you learn more about North Carolina.

INDEX

ABOUT THE AUTHOR
Katie Marsico has written more than 80 books for young readers. She hopes to one day relocate from the Midwest to the Southeast.